Be my sin. I'll be yours.
Let's hide in the shadows,
our only ally.
So we can let this fire burn
high and wild.
It's ok love, no one will
ever know, even though our
hands will memorize each
other's shapes.
Even though your tongue
will recall my taste when
you least expect.
Your saliva like a dose of
the most addictive drug I
will come to desperately
need.

Sin.

Just walk away love, pretend I don't exist, avoid my gaze.
Make them believe you do not know the taste of such craving.
I do not want human nor shadow to know about us so nothing can taint
this precious, illicit feeling.
All I want is to sin, and sin, and sin while pressed under your weight so
I can burn you into my memory for those lonely moments when I can't
have you.
They sleep beside us, oblivious.
Meanwhile in our dreams we are far away. Your finger twisting a dark curl
in my hair as I drowse away serenaded by the drumming
of your beating heart.

Dreams

You are my madness, my
inspiration
My alpha and most probably
my omega
The silent scream in the pit of
my stomach
The pain that hurts so good
The thorn in my flesh hurting
me as I smile
My most beautiful prayer
The sea breeze that warms me
one day
Only to make me shiver the
next
My Everest
The holder of the key to my
heart
Where this love lies
So beautiful yet so restless
Half joy, half torment
It quietens down until your
eyes drag me again, without
mercy
You are my song, my dream, my
fantasy and also my reality
Envelop my aching shape in
your arms
This love no longer being
seeded out in words
But whispered in your ears
Your breath blowing life into
me
When the fire takes over
Don't fear, step in
My flames burn deep
But the pain is so, so sweet.

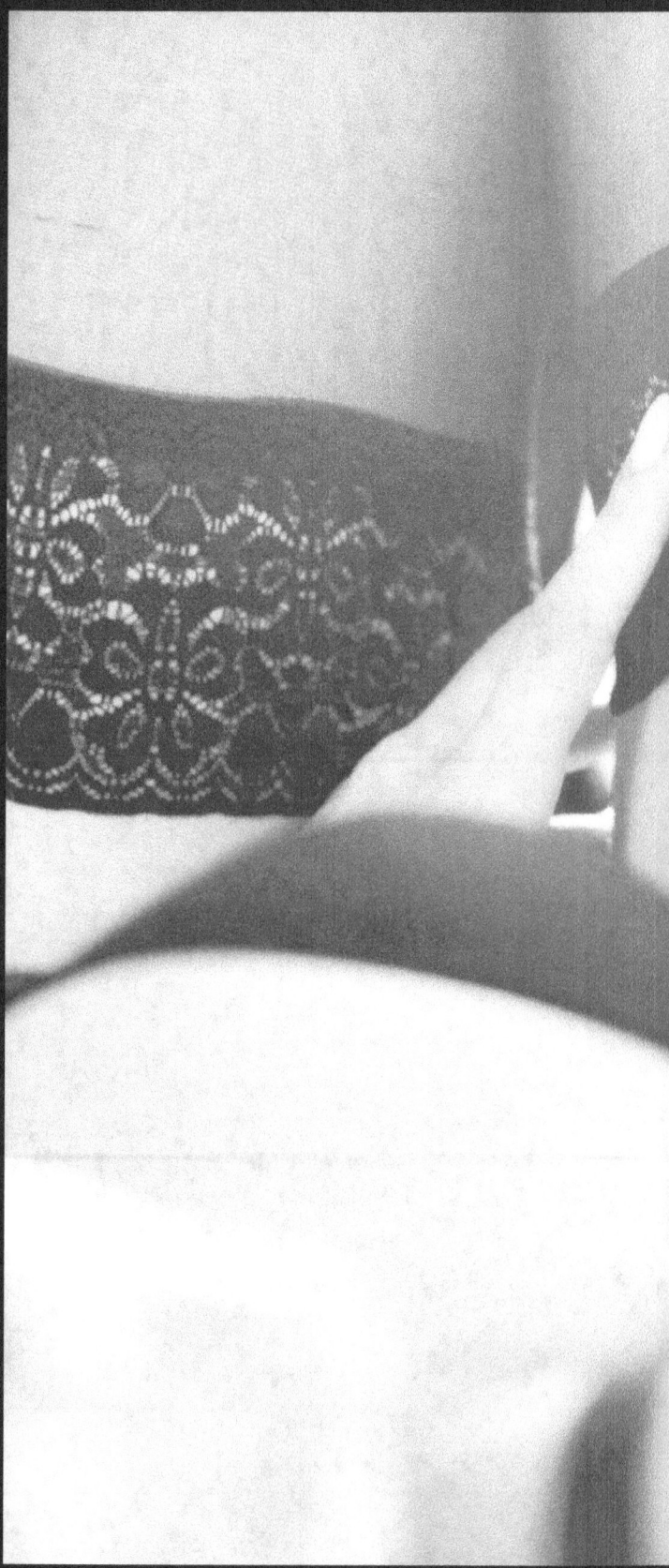

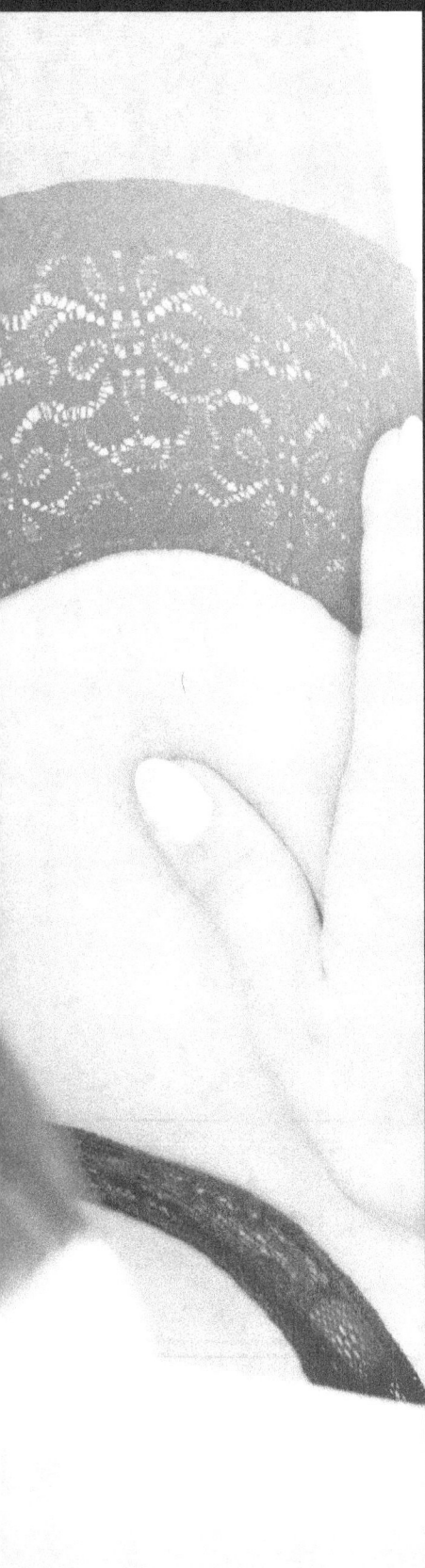

In case you need me I'm in that crowded room reserved to the ones who are cursed to love in vain.
That room where a glimpse of sunlight is but a dream dreamt years ago.
Surprisingly, Hope insists on lingering inside,
Perhaps the only emotion that is palpable,
Everything else is an illusion.
The flowers that bloom without scent.
The smell of you a musky creation of my latent desire.
Your misty kisses promising but never delivering.
Illusions that I choose to hold dear.
One day I might break the glass and cross the mirror to the other side where reality resides, but not tonight.
Tonight I want to be here, loving you, unavoidably hurting myself in the process.

I had a dream.
One of those that awaken you with a taste of reality.
A dream of candles lit with their golden glow blending with the hue of your skin.
My ravenous eyes feasting on your sinewy silhouette, muscles, hairs.
The overwhelming, unmistakable desire flushing your complexion.
Your throbbing flesh oozing love.
My lips swell and reach to claim what you so eagerly offer.
I wake up tasting salt, the warmth of your skin still in my mouth.

Illusions

Desire

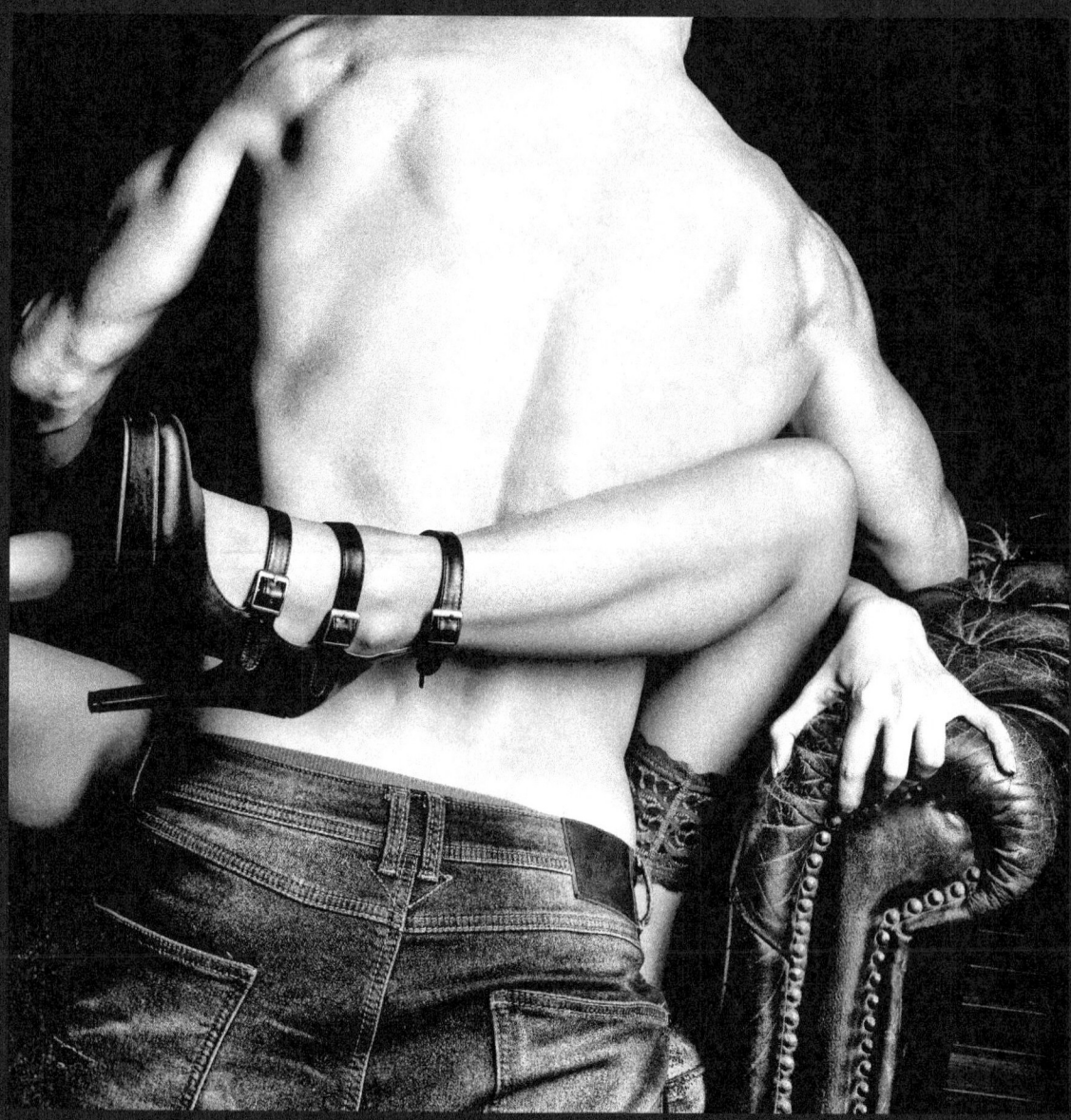

Your sweat on my tongue
Sending signals of lust
straight to my brain.

The current burning its
way down.
I lasso you between my
legs,
hard flesh, trembling flesh,
warm flesh.

The forbidden happening
between whispers and
moans.

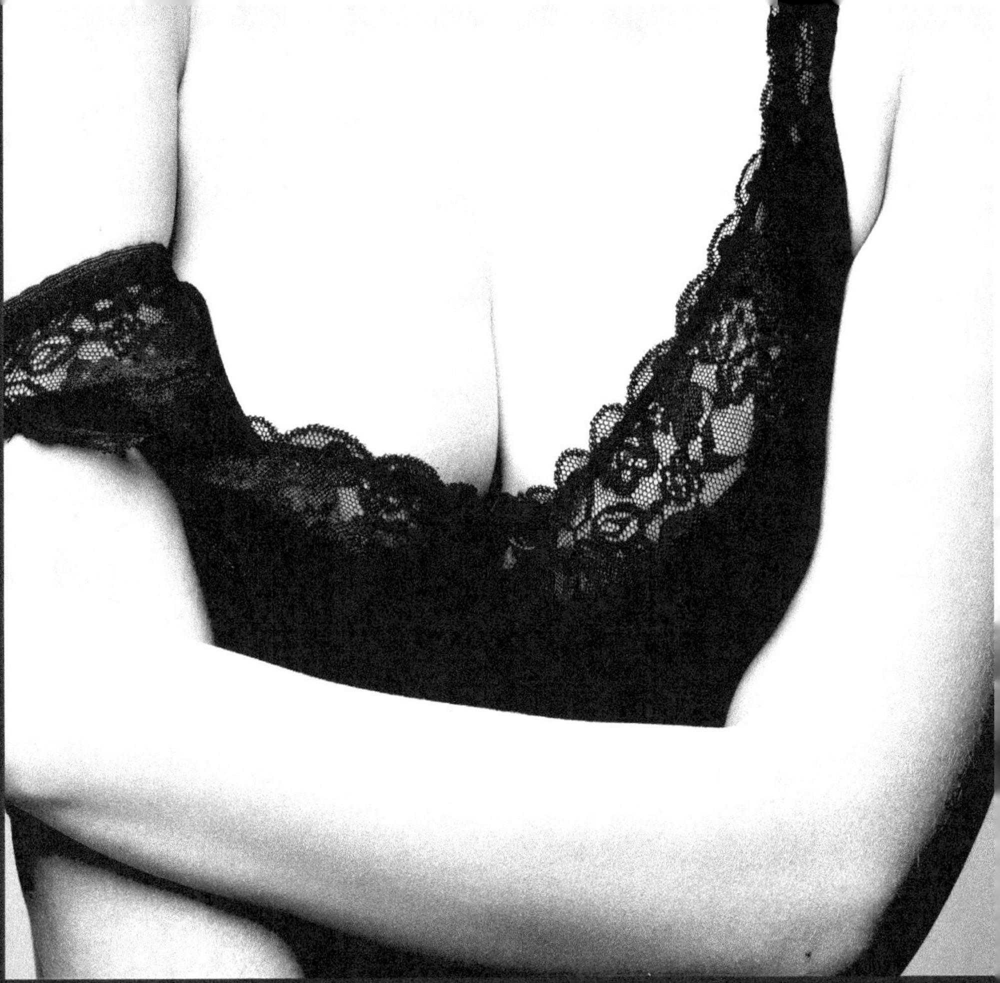

We fuck

unapologetically

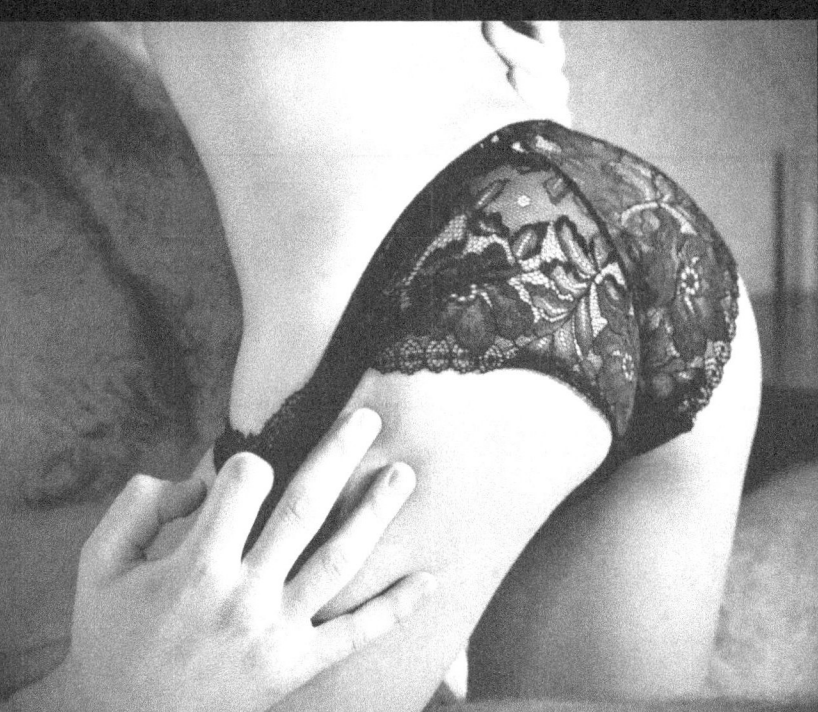

"Have you ever wanted to please
a man so much you were actually
scared you are going to lose notion
of who you are?"

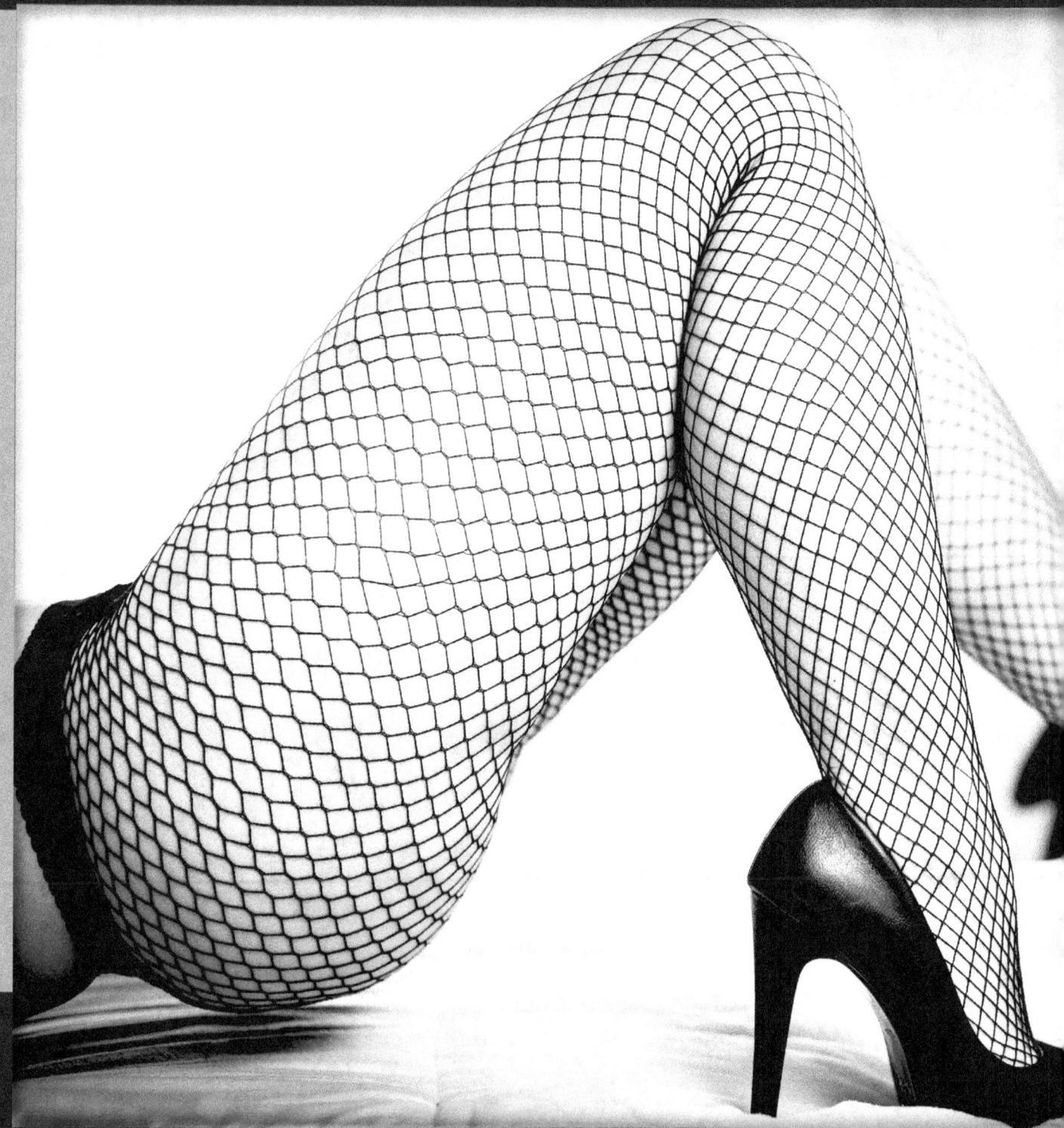

Yearning

*these dreams i dream of
hands grasping sheets
teeth biting pillows,
muffled sounds testing
the bedroom acoustics,
eyes rolling and bodies
that can't get close
enough
these dreams i dream
of craving flesh and
audacious hands and
melting loins, locking
legs and sweats
combined into an
alchemical miracle*

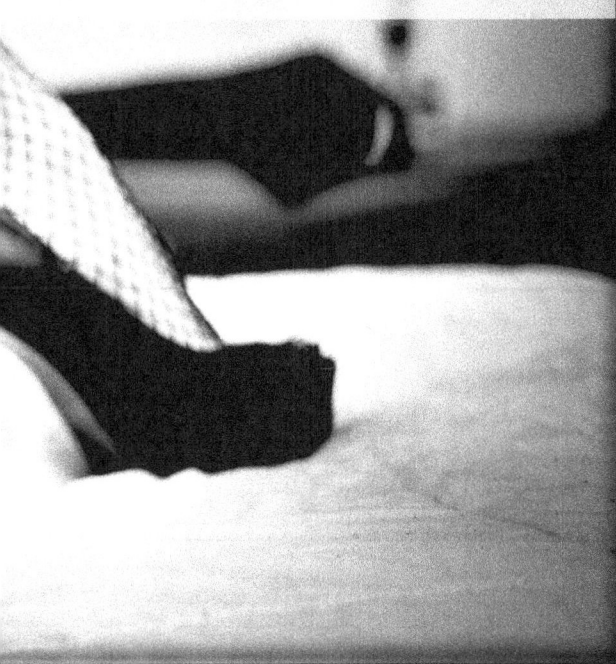

Look at the Moon tonight. Dancing in the sky like a lascivious orb, offering her light indiscriminately. Calling lovers to strip their clothes and shed their skin. Daring feverish bodies to mingle, tangle, reveal their hidden secrets.

That Moon up there, pirouetting courtesan she is, mocking me. I accept her challenge. The animal in me responds. Fire flows in and through. The invitation open. Trembling, feverish flesh desiring your hands. The sweet touch of your lips. My turn to mock the Moon. I smile back at her, smug in the knowledge of what I am about to do. She glows brighter, daring me. I close my eyes to see you in all your entirety. Flesh, scent, touch. You are not a dream. You are just him. And that's all I want you to be. You part me, you conquer me like a newfound land. The delirious feeling of your length exploring my every corner. Passionate. Relentless. Merciless. Repeatedly. My body shudders with such power and my lips cry your name with such abandonment that even the Moon, that big old pro, envies me. Because in that particular moment I shine brighter.

I want you to love me.

I am not your little sister. Nor am i your friend. Spare me the manners. Don't be a gentleman. Be all man. Want me with all you've got. The hunger of centuries. Act by instinct. Your heart pumping blood to places that make you forget you ought to resist. Desire taking you where you should not go. Lips yearning to taste the smell of ripe female flesh your nostrils picked up from me.

Don't be polite. Eat with your hands. Drink until you are intoxicated and can't wait another second.

Your hunger so out of control you need to lose yourself inside of me to be able to find a way out of the torment.

Don't be gentle.

Squeeze.

Bruise.

Bite.

Don't make love to me.

Fuck me like your life is about to end and i am the last pleasure you will ever have.

I want the devil in you to meet my darkest places until our fire combine and burn in unison and we can't tell who is who in our tangled mess.

We will explode in moans and cries and stars.

Then gather your breath, nest your head on my breasts.

God bless us. God bless the sin and redeem us in the name of love.

I will whisper a prayer into your ear, kiss your eyes and breathe new life into your heart so you can always find me.

In dreams. In life. In eternity.

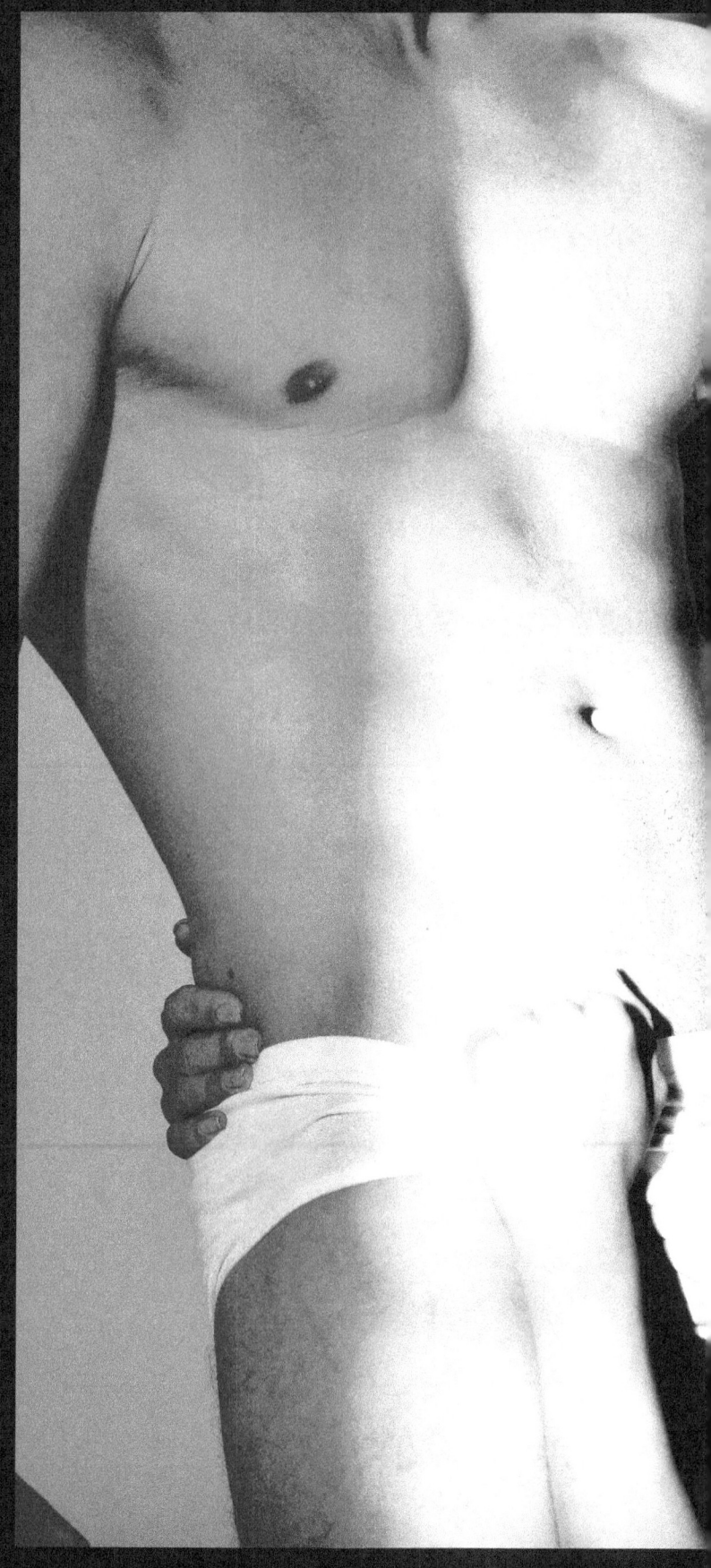

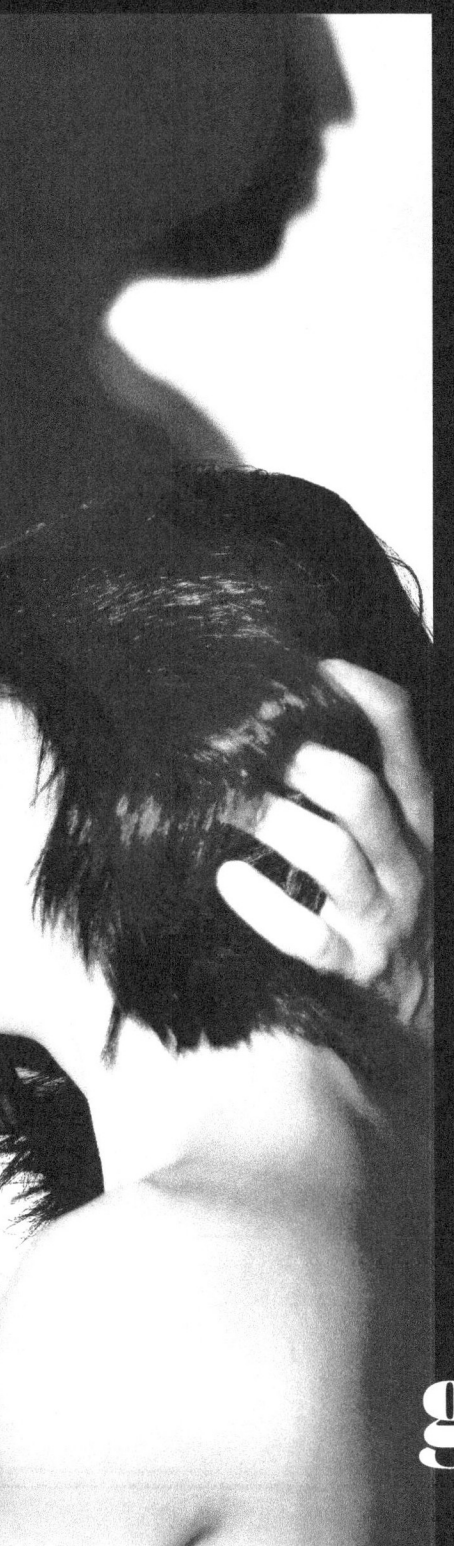

Lust.

It's like drowning. You wouldn't understand because I can't understand either. It's like the tide. I know it's coming but there's no raft or life jacket. I'm stranded. Waiting. And it comes and it's warm and it feels so right, until the air deserts me and I find myself unable to breathe. I panic but I know surrendering is the only way. So I remain still, listening to my heartbeat drumming your name until I drown in this poison I call Love. And I thank you for the sweetness with my very last breath.

greed

There are tender secrets ready to be revealed the exact moment your hand cups my breast, your finger finds the fork between my legs and your tongue demands mine.

Pleasure

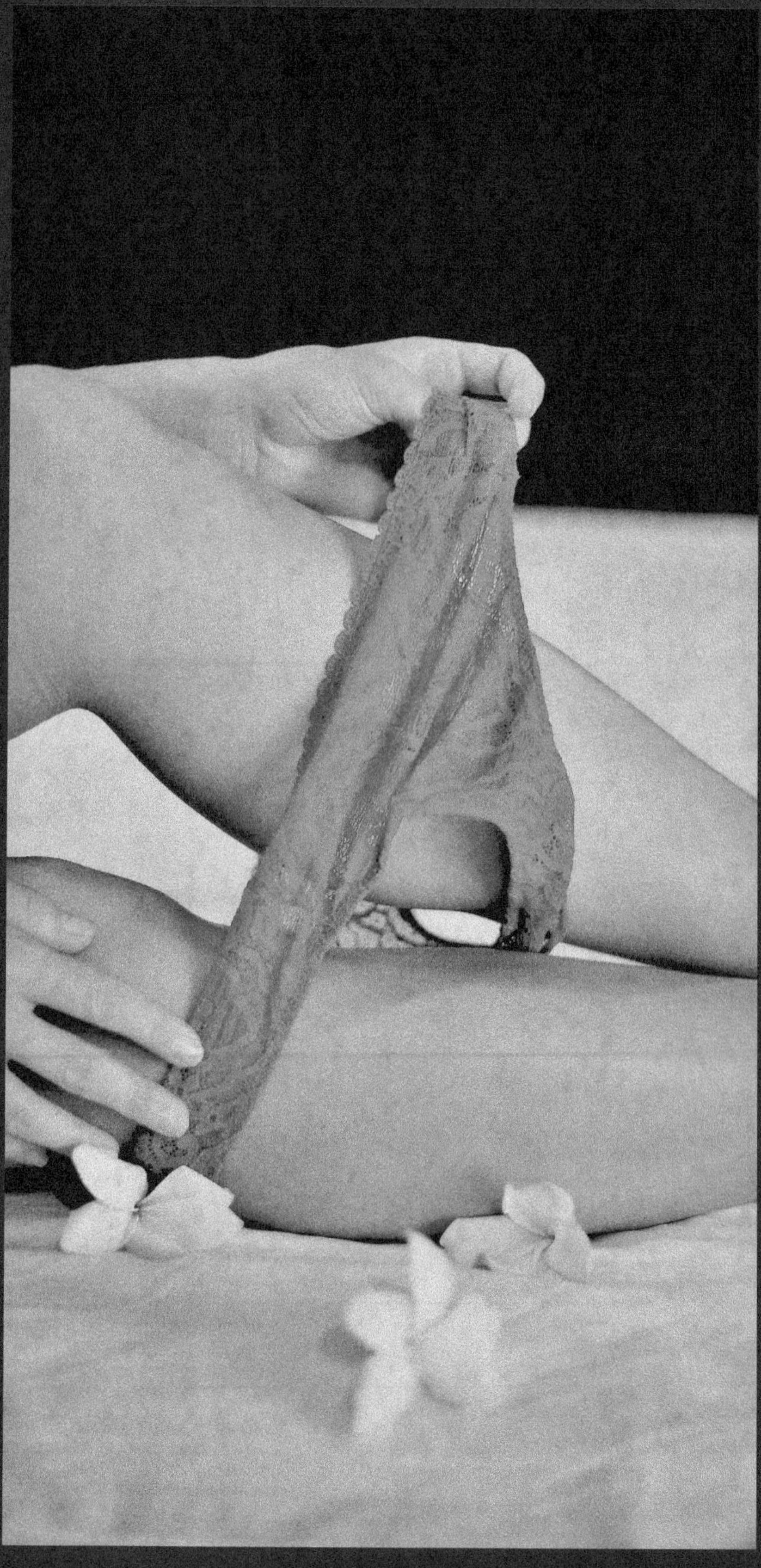

As simple as the smell of your breath in mine. That velvety feel of your lips and my greedy sucking of the wine from your saliva straight into my mouth. Drunk with you I close my eyes and open myself. The hard yet gentle pressure. The sweet ache inside amplifying the deeper you go. A gasp. Eyes meet eyes. I whimper. You groan. I don't know where I end and you begin. You are ruthless. I can't take it. I fly as high as an ungodly angel and explode into a million shades of ecstatic pleasure as I rain all over you.

How dare we glow so bright?

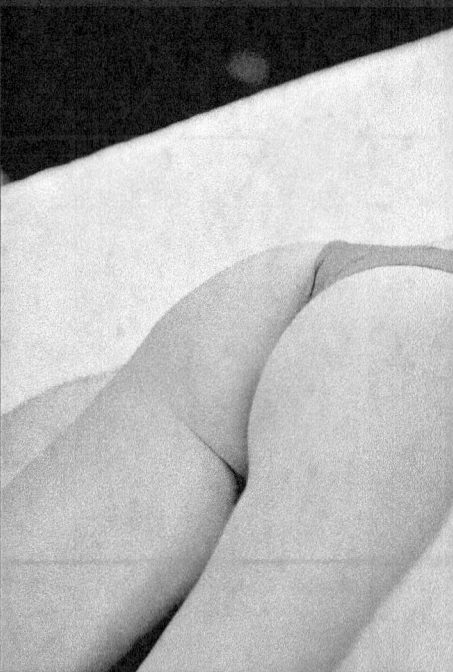

Break me baby. Like a wild animal you like the look of and take home out of curiosity. Study me. Probe me. Poke me. Push my buttons. Do little things that make me writhe, make me wince, make me smile, make me gasp and make me cry in stunned confusion as to what that feeling is. Is it pleasure? Is it pain? Is it both? Kiss me. Bite me. Bruise me. Play with m e like a rag doll, love me to death.

The weight of your palm on my fair skin. The tug of your hands as you use my hair to steady yourself as you take me. Nothing is a sin. I need to be yours until I cease to be myself and transform into a being focused entirely on your pleasure, your desires, your demands. Only then I can truly be free, when I am totally enslaved to your love.

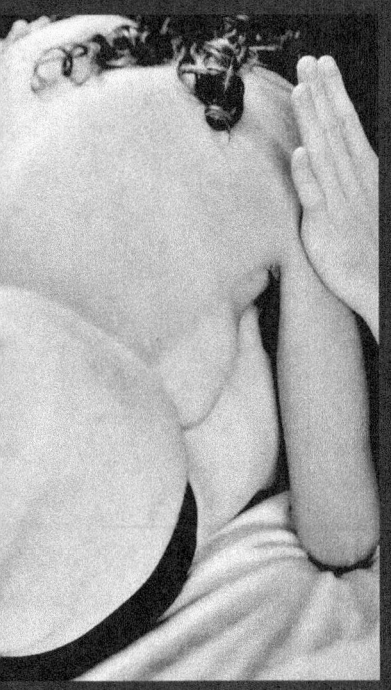

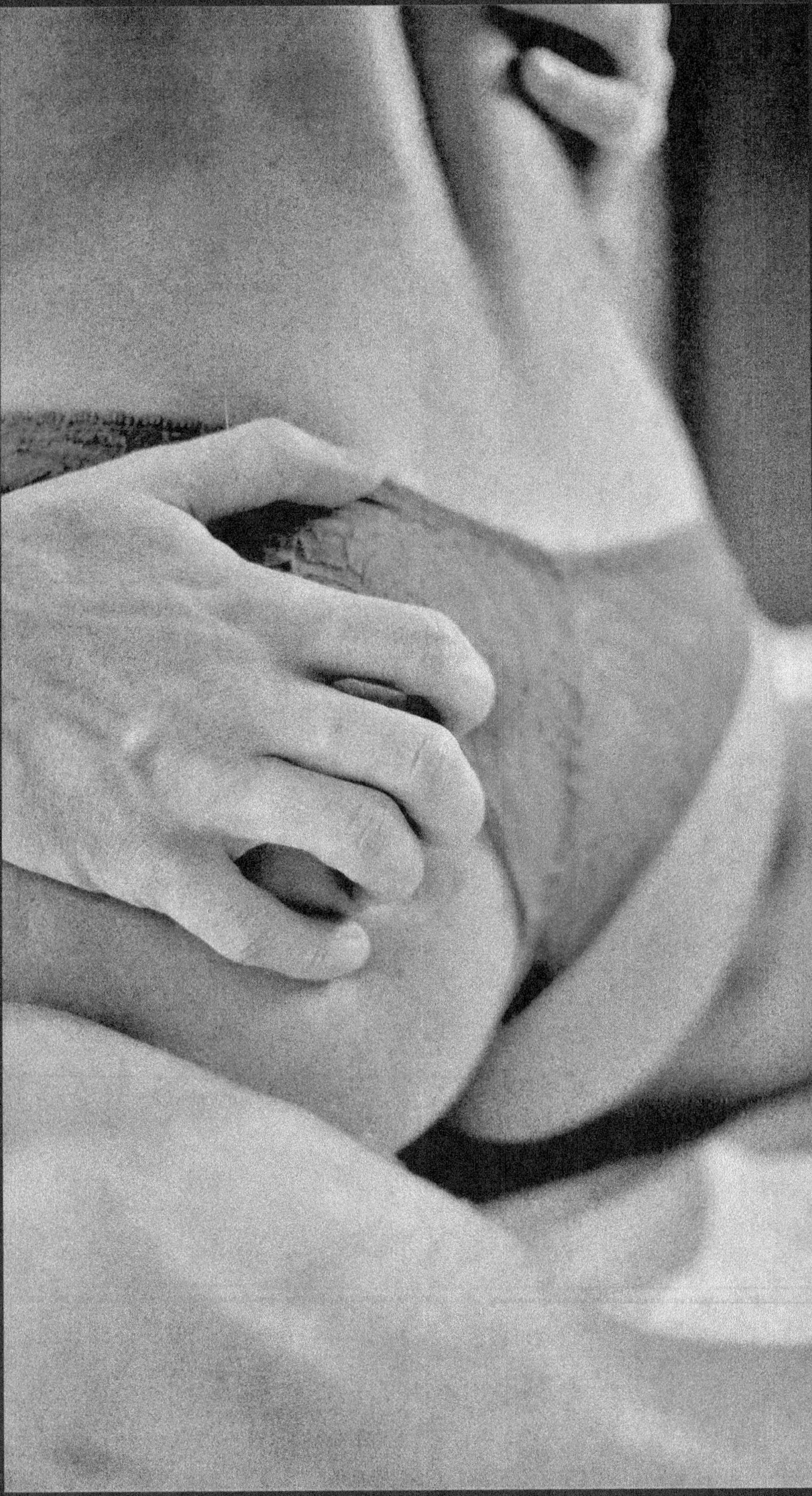

lovers.

Loving someone with such abandonment.
Offering yourself as a devotional sacrifice to such feeling.
Hear the ocean. Lie down on the sand and close your eyes.
You are completely at the mercy of the tide and the current.
You are hanging by one thread. You know it can swallow you whole and drown
you into despair. You can set yourself free but you choose to stay,
because the sugar secreted by your deepest fantasies of him is so sweet. And
the longing for his touch is so powerful you choose to give more and more
love. Never returned for love is free.
Here comes the tide...

Surrendering

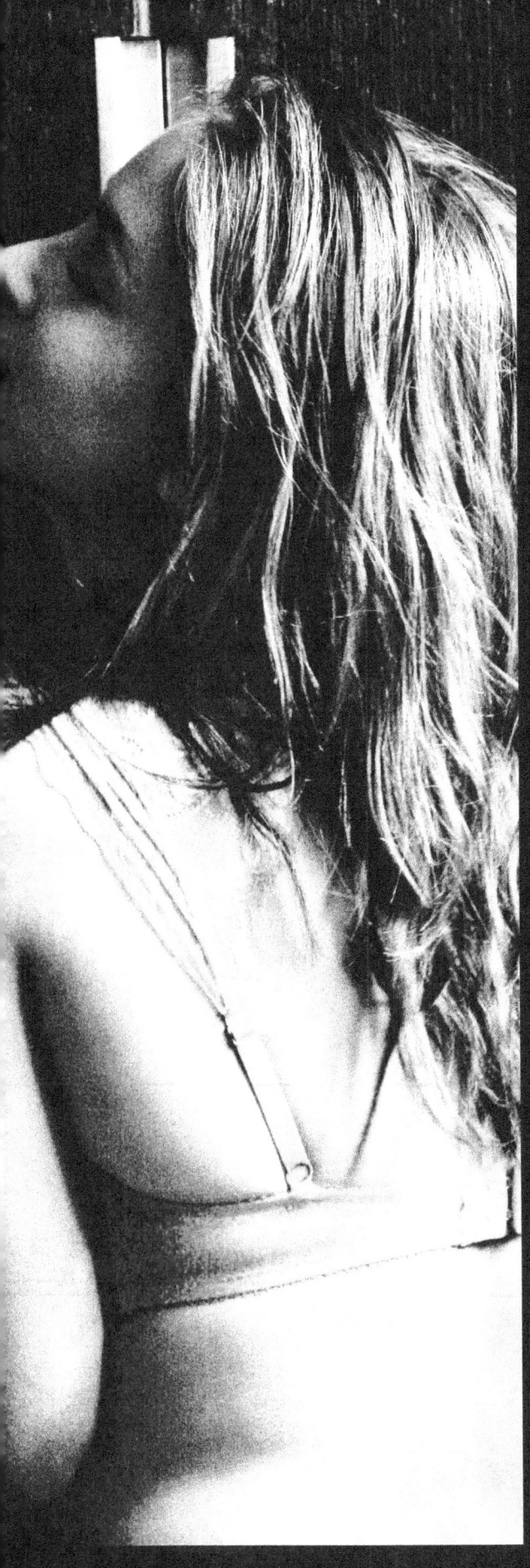

There's this kind of love that's akin to a chronic malady, an ache, a travesty. It exists in you not like an outside feeling that entered when you were distracted but it seems to be part of your core. It is not made of hands intertwined but of a resolute acceptance of a never to be, never to touch.

The tragedy of such love is the ever unfulfilled desire, the hunger, that familiar ache inside. It's a craving that won't subside. A perpetual abstinence. It robs you from your sleep. It brings on dreams that feel real, waking you up with the trail of fire down the skin where his lips have just been. The body starved, the mind stunned, love rushing from your heart to every corner of your being. Waves destined not to crash. Ripples of frustrated desire. It's no use to ignore the need.

While your image is still vivid I take your hand to where it hurts the most, the pain coming to a crescendo until it no longer belongs to me.

Sweet Torture

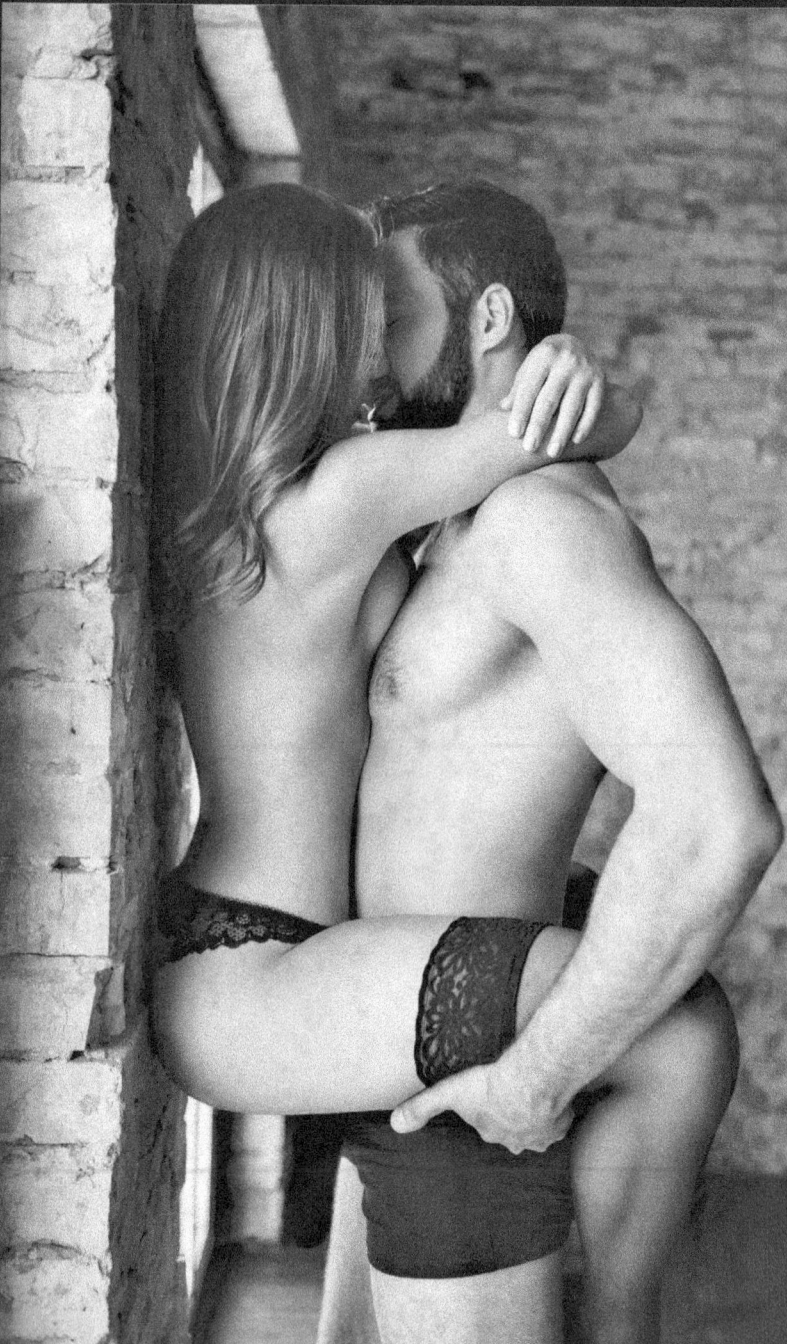

There is no measure for love, desire, tenderness.
The heart identifies the other by sight, scent, instinct.
A chemical reaction begins. The heart accelerates. The body tingles. The core aches begging for relief.
There is no measuring. Just giving in, allowing the waves to hit the shore over and over,
leaving ripples of unsung serenades. Unspoken feelings.
A vat of the sweetest wine of the best vintage.
Contained.
Untried.
Untouched.
Full to the brim. Ready to spill.

burn with me

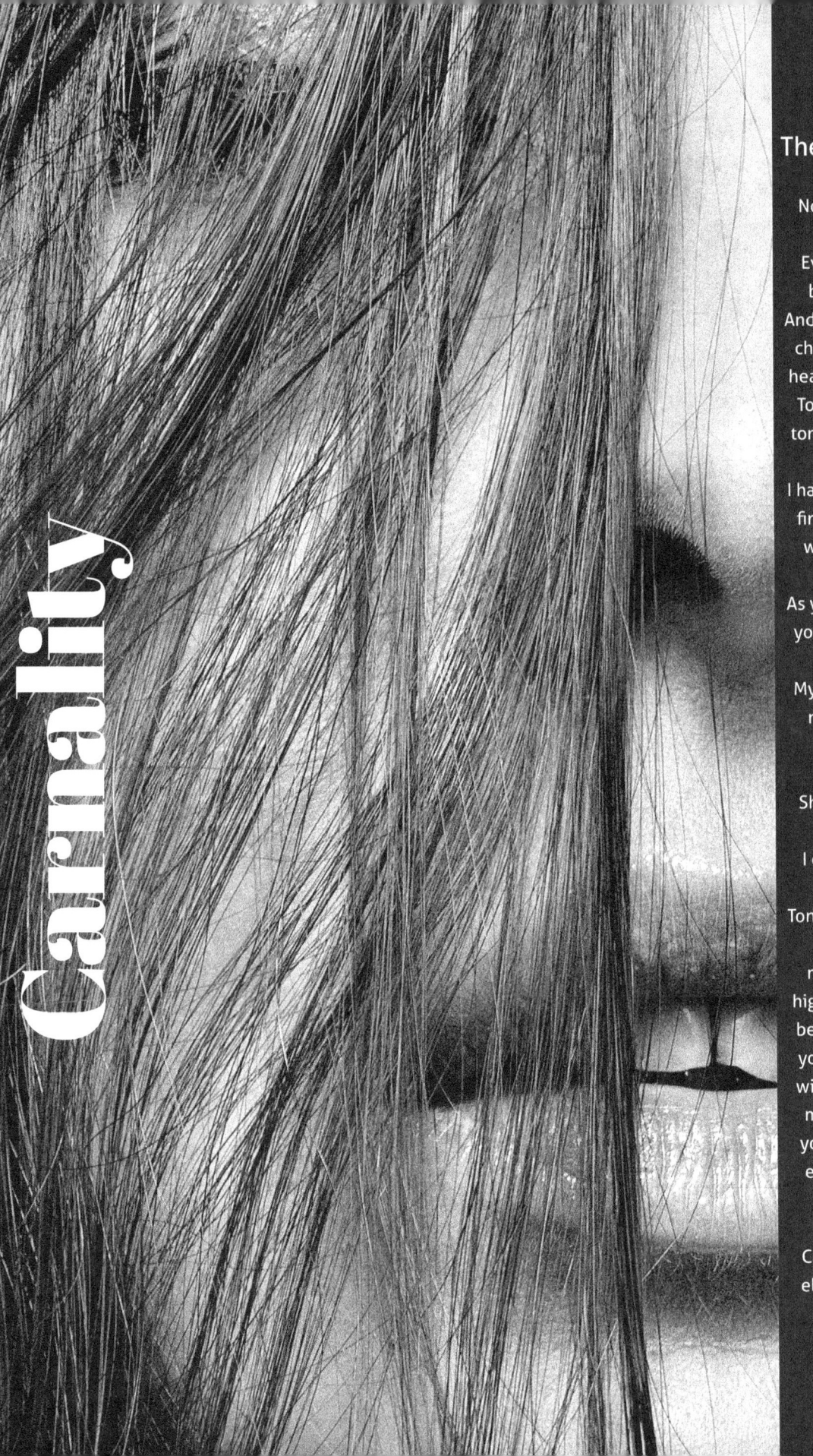

Carnality

The Dream is mine.

No one is to tell me what goes.
Everything in this Castle built in the air is mine.
And I feel like laying on your chest tonight to hear your heart drumming in my ears.
Tonight I will devour your tongue, taste your lips, kiss you long and deep.
I have the need to suck your fingers and guide them to where I'm aching to feel them.
As you find me I'll moan into your mouth while nibbling your lips.
My breath caught between not quite there and the explosion that comes seconds after.
Shaken I search for you in the dark.
I embrace your body and soul.
Tonight you will take me like you own me,
make me weak, take me high up to the clouds until I beg for release, then allow yourself to explode in me, with me, until the smile on my face gets etched into your memory and tears of ecstasy stream down my face,
Because tonight, in my Castle, you have nowhere else to be but in my arms.

Here you are dancing in my mind. You voice going around like a prayer lulling my core into disarray. The insanity of the desire to have you with me, in me. Hands that neglect gentleness, pleading breathless whispers, sweat dripping from your forehead into my mouth. I taste the salt right before your ravenous lips take mine. The salt turning into toffee on my tongue. Lingering. Wild, untamed, mad desire. You rearranging my insides. Who are you? Who am I? Does it matter?

I am no longer who I was when you started. The waves inside gaining momentum, the undercurrent taking me. Where? Could this be Heaven? My Spirit soars, freed by you. I am part me, part animal, part ether. I hold on to you because I am inebriated by the ride, so high I am afraid to fall. I am no longer in control. Surely, there can't be another level to your claim, and yet you take me further. I tighten up and take all you are so willingly offering. You let go. I am your death and your rebirth. You are my ritual and my connection to God. Together we are poetry.

Passion

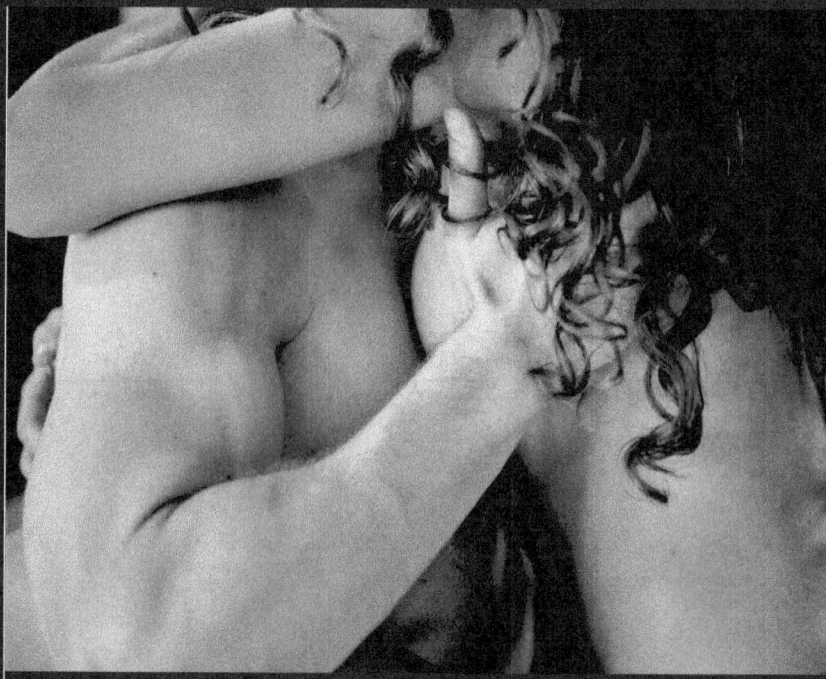

Poison. Sweet, exquisitely addictive poison.
I stand at the door of doom, drinking your features.
Love zombie I am totally stunned by your eyes.
I am a shell for you to fill up with more of your intoxicating love.
I no longer live, I love.
Watch me love, licking my lips, famished, awaiting for the next dose.

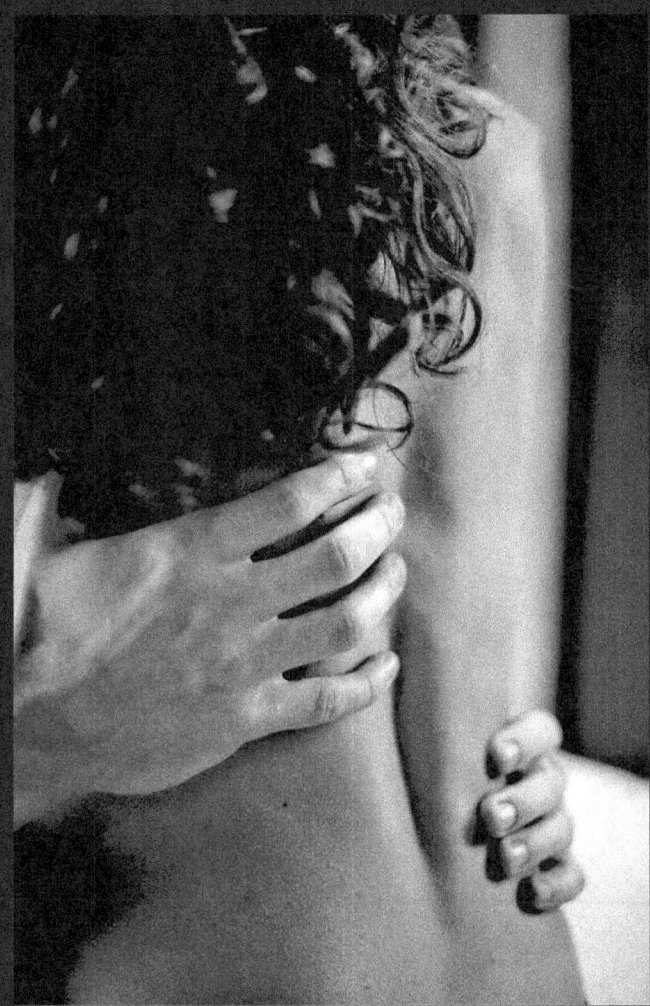

Defying all the laws of Space and Time Neptune takes the Sun out for a dance.
Like Stars colliding in the navy sky.
Him in blue shades of water, his shy nature betraying itself out of fascination.
Her a spiraling fire bomb putting on a majestic display, warming up the path towards him.
Her inquisitive nature. His caution. Her impulsiveness. His reservation. Still they touch and sizzle, Water and Fire coming together.
She's scared he will obliterate her. He's scared she will consume him. Instead
Her fire warms him in ways he didn't know he needed. His cool stream soothes her in ways she didn't think possible.
And just like that the impossible happens,
and the sky is none the wiser, the Moon illuminating their forbidden love.

Unrestrained

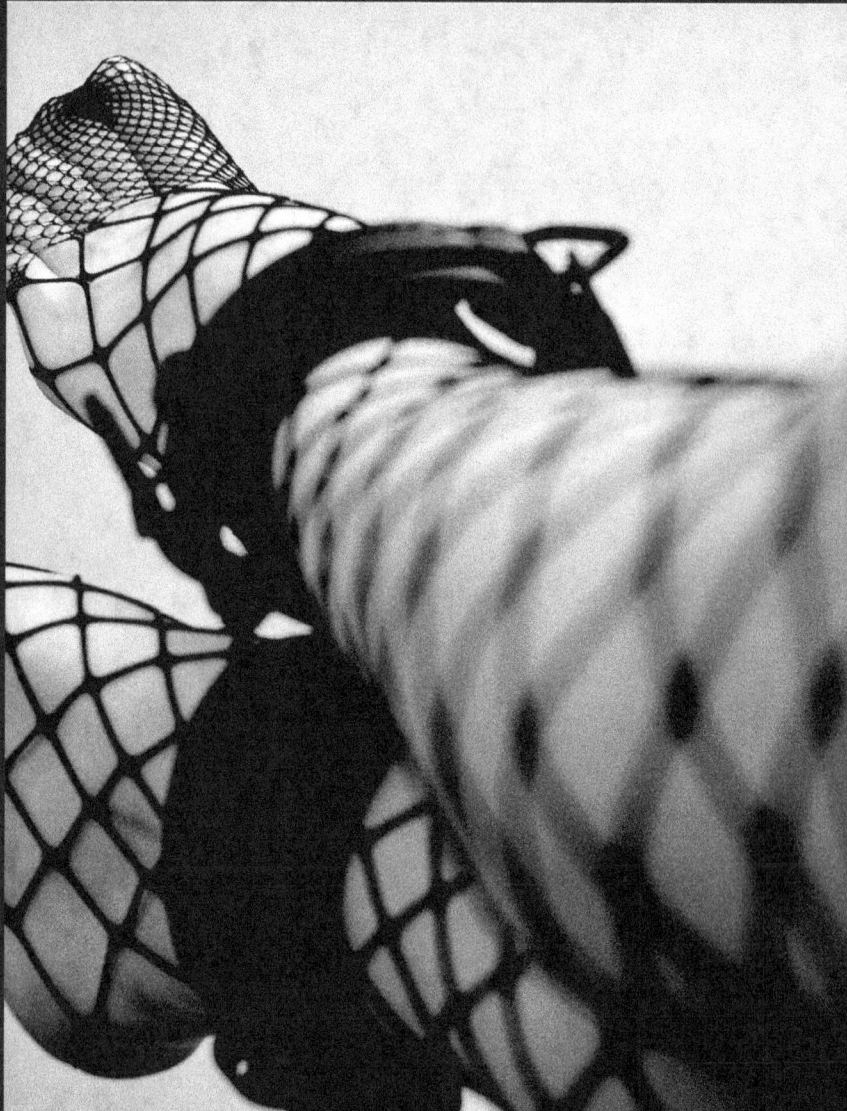

Profane

Are you scared? Don't be, my love.
I would not mine the fortress you built around yourself. I would not step on the flowers on your garden. I would not ask you to split yourself in half or offer what you cannot give. I would simply want to be that unexpected smile out of place at the wrong time. That longing that hits you out of nowhere. The smell that awakens your passion. The memory of hands on your skin setting it on fire.
The kiss you crave when your desire surfaces. The excitement of time ticking as you anticipate that sweetness on your tongue late at night when no one is watching. That irresistible torment of your flesh that makes your thoughts and your hands wander.
The warmth you want to be buried in.
The fire you want to be consumed in until there is nothing left but our exhausted breaths in each other's mouths.

Your daydream.

Your sin.

Your secret.

Your plaything.

HUSH NOW.
Your lips have a job to do

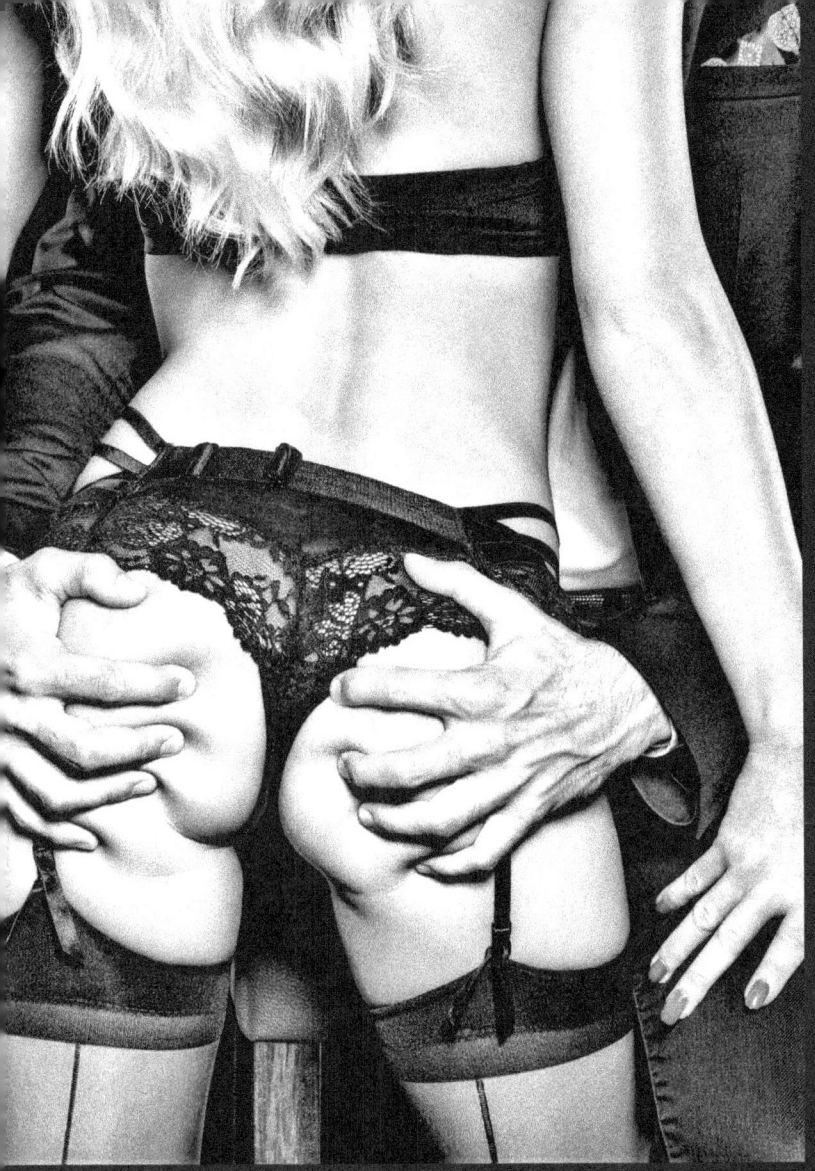

Stop the madness in me by taming the wild, thirsty beast that salivates for the taste of your love. Bind me, subdue me, beat me in my own game. Put me in my place by forcing your weight upon my body. Shut me up with your hungry lips, scratch my delicate skin with your stubble. Pry me open as roughly as you can muster. Enter me uninvited, my eager sex betraying my flimsy pretended resistance. Ravished, taken, conquered. I lay bare as you look to find your own relief inside of me. The wildness in your eyes subsiding with every thrust. Our bodies locked together in the most primal fight. We both surrender to our need, our instincts, to greedily taking and sacredly giving. In you I find me, for pleasing you is my purpose. In me you find love, solace, a home away from home. Together we are beautiful.

SILENCE NOW. HEAR THE CURRENT RUNNING THROUGH ME. ARE YOU THIRSTY? CLOSE YOUR EYES, OPEN YOUR SENSES. FIND ME BY SCENT. I AM BUT A BUD DRIPPING NECTAR. UNEARTH ME. UNCOVER MY SECRET. PART ME. THE POUNDING ROSY FLESH BLOSSOMING AT YOUR INSPECTION. RELIEVE THE PLEADING CLAMOR OF MY CORE BETWEEN YOUR LIPS. MY BODY RETURNING THE TORTURE IN MUFFLED SOBS. THE VELVET OF YOUR LIPS ON MY TENDER FLESH. YOUR HANDS AND THEIR FIRM GRASP ON MY THIGHS, OPENING, EXPOSING. THE TORMENT MAKING ME CONVULSE. OH LOVE, FOR A MOMENT YOU ARE MY TORMENTOR AND MY SAVIOUR. I OOZE LOVE, YOU DRINK WITH THE THIRST OF SAILORS. HOW SWEET TO DIE IN YOUR MOUTH, YOUR HANDS LEAVING BRUISES ON MY FAIR SKIN. YOUR FAST BREATHING SLOWLY STEAMING MY THIGHS.

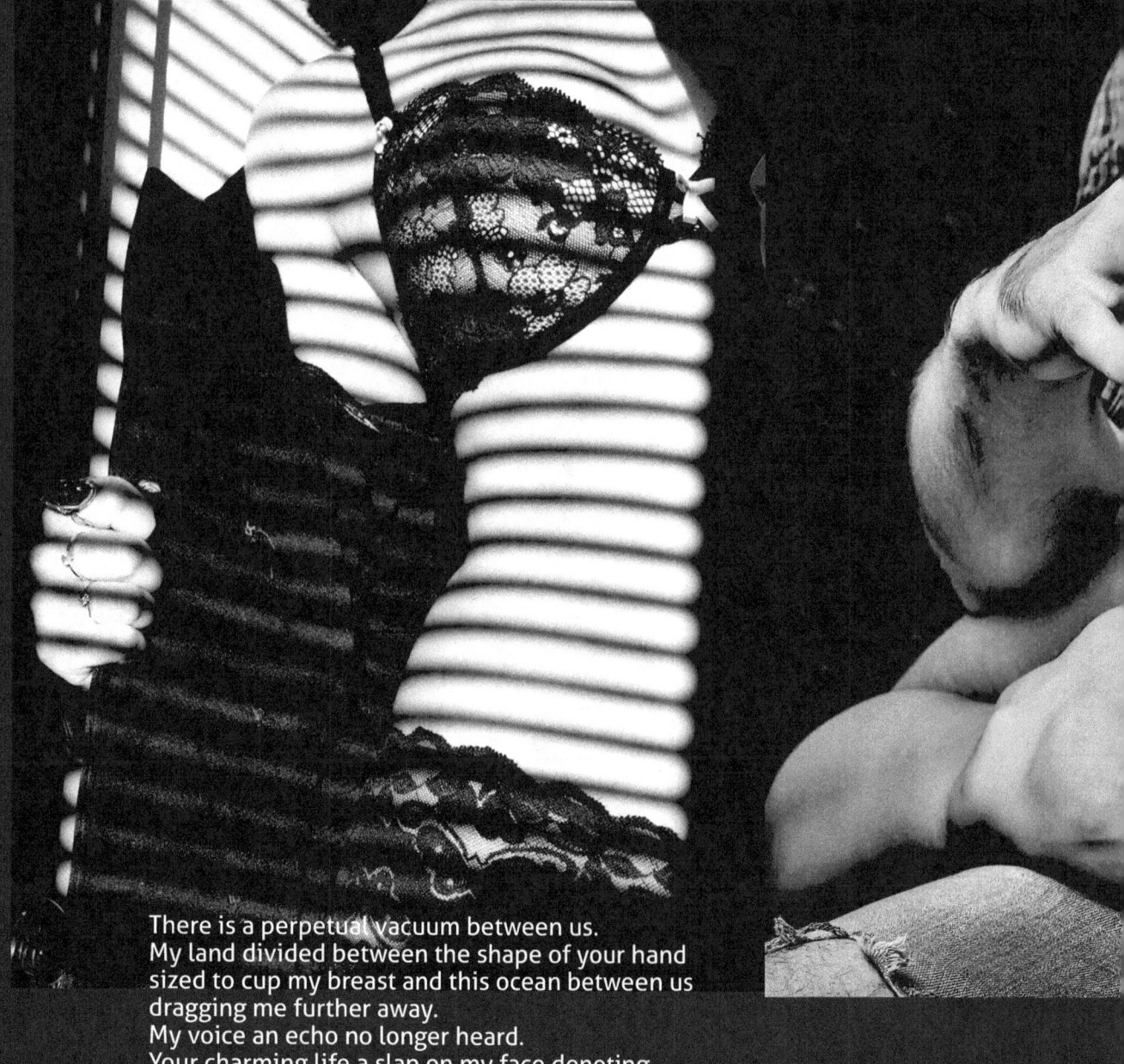

There is a perpetual vacuum between us.
My land divided between the shape of your hand
sized to cup my breast and this ocean between us
dragging me further away.
My voice an echo no longer heard.
Your charming life a slap on my face denoting
how needed I am not.
The flesh still branded by your touch bringing
back a sigh. My own brain censoring my
weakness.
The undeniable need to bloom at your gaze like
a spring flower deprived of warmth. The blushing
of these cheeks that know damn well what the
cost is but still cannot bear to avert your gaze.
Shameful fool I am for I know it takes only one
word from your lips to silence my being. 'Come' -
you say. And God forgive me...I will. Every single
time.

Take me.

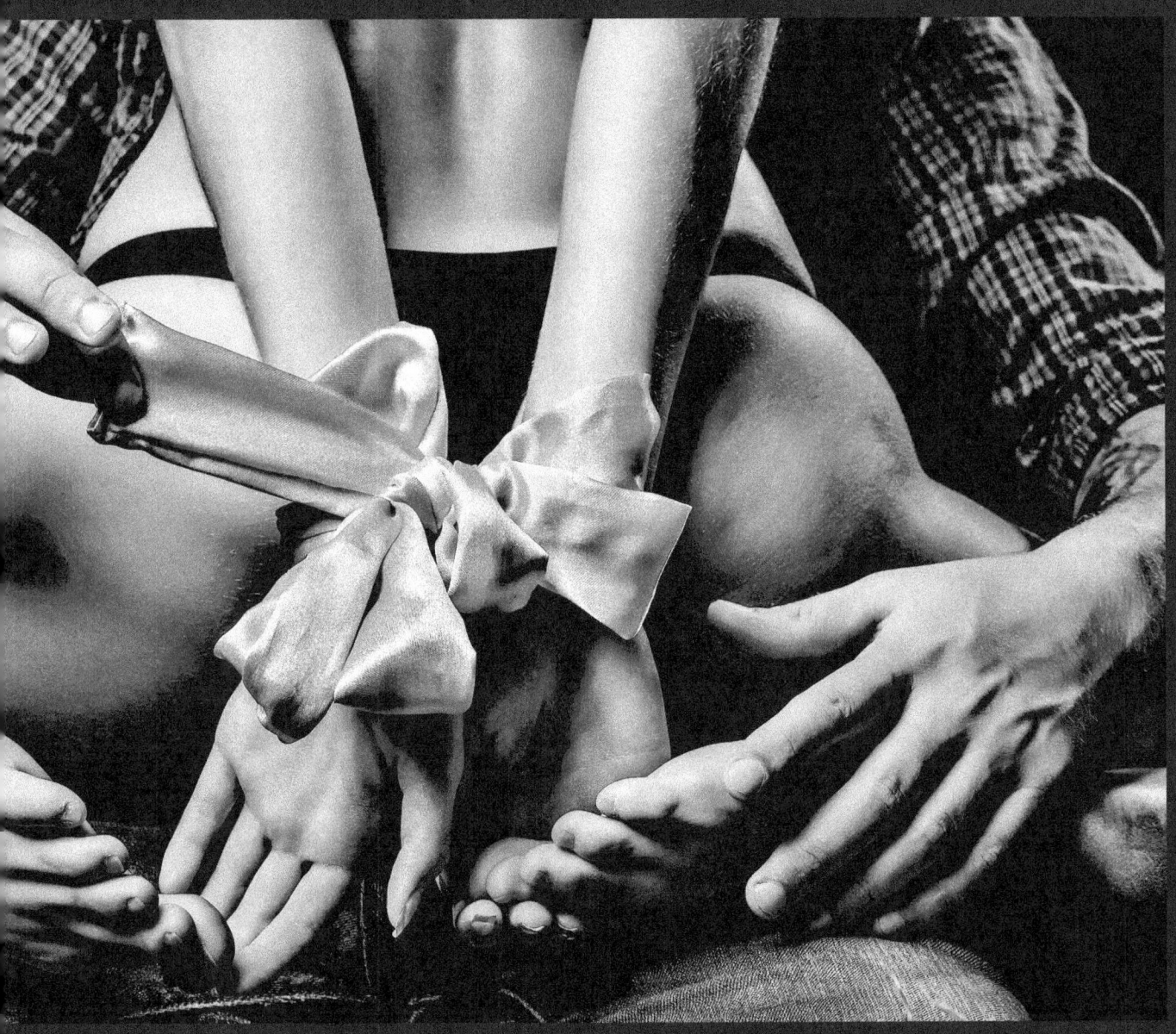

You are no stranger to me. I remember your taste. Was it a dream? A fragment of another life? Or was it real? Whatever it was I sorely miss that taste. You reduce me to longing and waiting. For another dream, another life, another reality.

Let the world crumble around us. Who cares about the latest news, the bills and the plagues, the bad and the ugly. The protests, the tyrants and their stupidity. Here in this room nothing is allowed, just you and the thirst of your lips sucking my flesh and the writhing of my body as you take me to Heaven. Just me and the rhythm of my hips pulling you in, your moment of extreme rapture completely buried in my warmth. We join the stars in their beauty and matter-of-factness. We are. The rest is dust to be swept under the rug. Pushed aside. Forgotten.

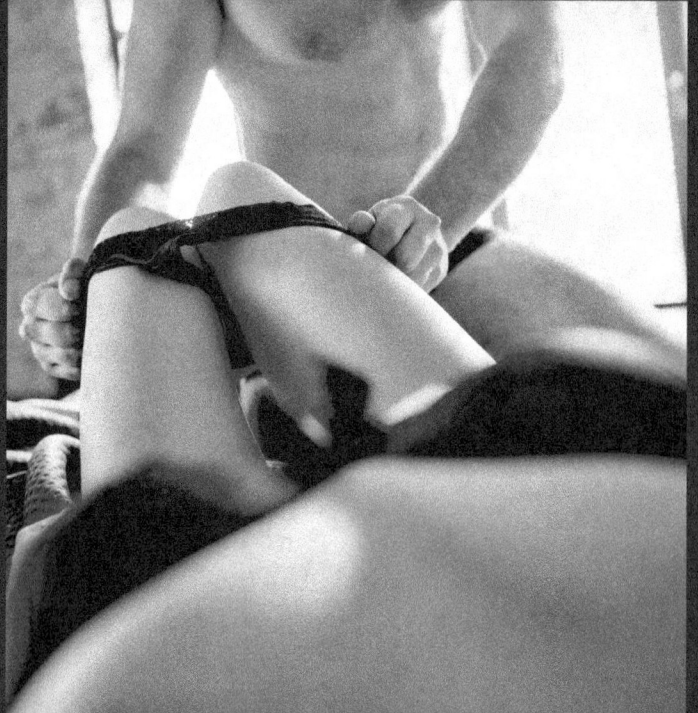

Can you bury your fingers in me as I melt onto your hands and drip onto the carpet? Can you make me beg? Use my mouth as you see fit?
Love, can you fuck me so hard I actually forget who I am? Reduce me to your lover, your bitch, your slave. Sting me and I will thank you as you lovingly kiss the red shape of your palm on my skin.

Can you push me against the wall
Shut me up with your lips
Make me wince as you dig your fingers into my hair to make me understand who I belong to?
Can you demand I part my lips so your thumb can find its way in? Your fingers wet with my saliva, inspecting my mouth as if to check if it can comply with your plans for it.
Can you tell me that I'm being a good girl as I part my legs at your command?

Will you?

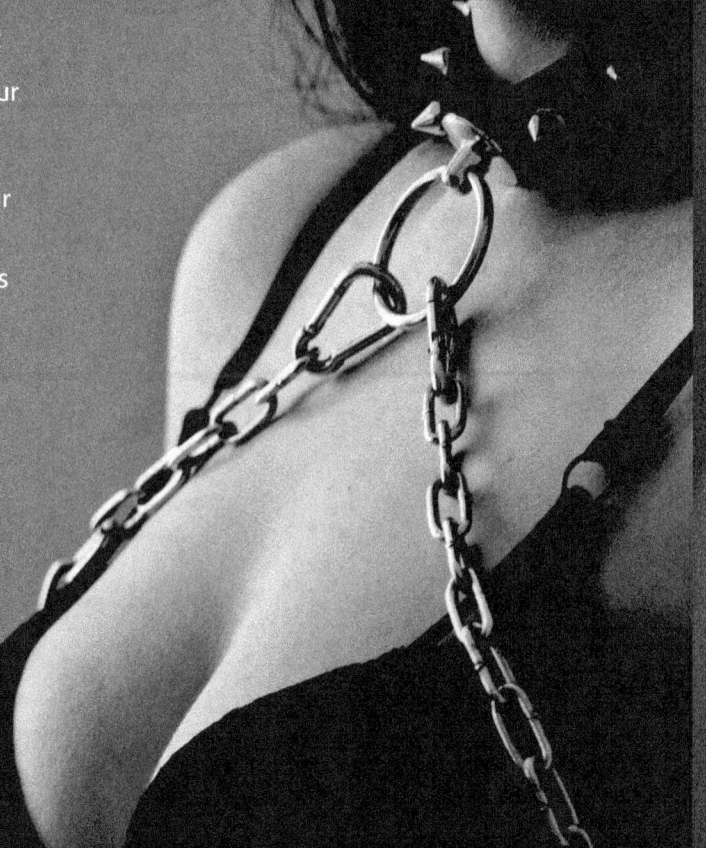

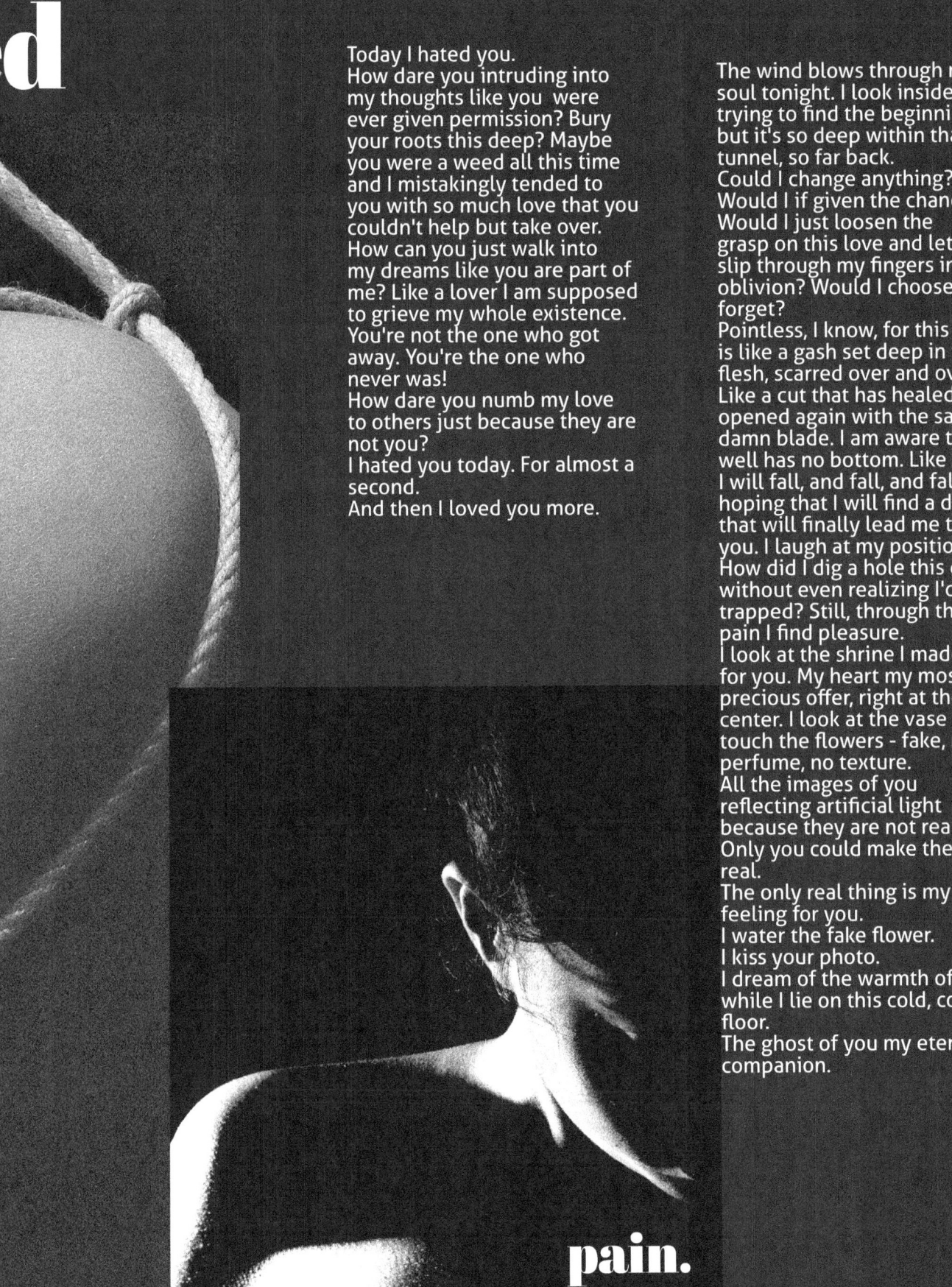

d

Today I hated you.
How dare you intruding into my thoughts like you were ever given permission? Bury your roots this deep? Maybe you were a weed all this time and I mistakingly tended to you with so much love that you couldn't help but take over.
How can you just walk into my dreams like you are part of me? Like a lover I am supposed to grieve my whole existence.
You're not the one who got away. You're the one who never was!
How dare you numb my love to others just because they are not you?
I hated you today. For almost a second.
And then I loved you more.

The wind blows through my soul tonight. I look inside trying to find the beginning, but it's so deep within that tunnel, so far back.
Could I change anything? Would I if given the chance? Would I just loosen the grasp on this love and let it slip through my fingers into oblivion? Would I choose to forget?
Pointless, I know, for this love is like a gash set deep in the flesh, scarred over and over. Like a cut that has healed and opened again with the same damn blade. I am aware this well has no bottom. Like Alice I will fall, and fall, and fall, hoping that I will find a door that will finally lead me to you. I laugh at my position. How did I dig a hole this deep without even realizing I'd be trapped? Still, through the pain I find pleasure.
I look at the shrine I made for you. My heart my most precious offer, right at the center. I look at the vase and touch the flowers - fake, no perfume, no texture.
All the images of you reflecting artificial light because they are not real. Only you could make them real.
The only real thing is my feeling for you.
I water the fake flower.
I kiss your photo.
I dream of the warmth of you while I lie on this cold, cold floor.
The ghost of you my eternal companion.

pain.

Ultimately. His.

Acknowledgments

To my inner self for believing I could.
For the young girl in me who kept the flame alive.
To the ones who understand my need to bleed in words
when I'm overwhelmed, impassioned and full of emotions
I can't even begin to explain, let alone contain.
To the gift of Words for being my safety zone and a true
companion throughout my life.
To all of my friends who encouraged me despite my
reservations.
And to my eternal inspiration, whose name I dare not say.
I'm still waiting for you. In a room at the end of the world
or some place as pedestrian as a hotel room. The magic
does not require matching surroundings. Our beating
hearts will suffice.

ANNA FLINT
POETRESS. WEAVER OF FANTASIES.

Anna Flint
Writer and Poetress.

annaflintwrites@gmail.com
IG: @annaflintwrites
annaflintwrites.com